ACTIVE MEDITATION FOR MANIFESTING THE KINGDOM

Celie Thomas

1st WORLD PUBLISHING

Active Meditation for Manifesting the Kingdom

Published by 1st World Publishing
P.O. Box 2211, Fairfield, Iowa 52556
tel: 641-209-5000 • fax: 866-440-5234
web: www.1stworldpublishing.com

Second Edition

LCCN: 2017915229

Softcover ISBN: 978-1-4218-3793-2

TABLE OF CONTENTS

INTRODUCTION

How difficult could it be? I had read and listened to many testimonials on the benefits of meditation; of quieting the mind and finding a deep, inner connection to God. Even Jesus spent time in isolation, seeking guidance and recharging his spirit. But in reality, the intellectual understanding of meditation and the act of meditating are worlds apart. One requires engaging the human mind while the other involves a willingness to open the spirit to the will of God with an attitude of joyful trust.

In 1986, with three children in elementary school and a husband who worked long hours, my decision to go to graduate school was as ignorant as it was ambitious. I had graduated from college eleven years earlier and taught elementary school for two years when my life took a sharp turn into full time motherhood. Now I wanted to pursue a degree in counseling and return to the elementary school setting as a professional school counselor. Besides the daunting task of juggling this new endeavor with the responsibilities of home and family, I was haunted by memories of "test phobia" and knew it could sabotage the entire effort. Friends suggested I try daily, scheduled meditation, but I soon realized that nothing short of a sensory deprivation tank could still the three-ring circus in my head.

What began as a simple, thirty-minute walk two or three times a week evolved into a very powerful, structured process that still helps me to "be still and know that (He is) God" (Ps.46:10). The most fascinating result of this practice is that the mind becomes conscious of the daily miracles of life on this planet, and the Kingdom of God is truly at hand at any given moment.

Active Meditation for Manifesting the Kingdom is a handbook of sorts for those who long for opportunities to reflect and meditate in uninterrupted peace, but whose busy lives lack such luxury. The "active meditation" process described in this book can actually happen any place and anytime. I do, however, recommend regular walking and occasional journaling of the insights and results that occur, as this most definitely enhances appreciation of God's work within and all around us.

CHAPTER ONE
BEGIN EACH DAY WITH PRAISE

Then I heard the voices of every creature in heaven and on earth and under the earth and in the sea; everything in the universe cried aloud:
"To the One seated on the throne, and to the Lamb, be praise and honor, glory and might, forever and ever!" (Rev. 5:13)

The hierarchy of the heavens has been a topic of discussion since the beginning of human communication, from early cave drawings to the development of spoken and written languages. And yet, in the final analysis, each individual has his or her own very personal belief system that is nearly impossible to explain to another individual. Faith communities may gather in song and scriptural recitation; and the power of concentrated prayer cannot be denied even by scientific standards. But each person's relationship with a Supreme Being -- God, our Source, or "the Universe" as some prefer to say -- is unique. I happen to believe that "the Lamb" referred to in the quoted verse refers to Jesus Christ, the Messiah, through whom our petitions to the Almighty are heard and fulfilled. Praise, therefore, begins for me with an invocation to Christ.

When I first began active meditation, it seemed like the least I could do was approach the Lord with the good manners afforded to the people in my life. I would never, for example, call someone up and begin to make demands on their time or energy without first expressing a positive salutation of some kind; even a word of appreciation for their presence in my life. It seemed logical, then, to begin a prayer dialogue with Christ by offering thanksgiving for his presence and the blessings in my life, preferably out loud. An example of "Praise" goes something like this:

Lord, Jesus Christ,

Thank you for this brand new day of life, right here and right now.

Thank you for your constant, guiding, loving presence in my life.

Thank you for (names of loved ones).

Thank you for blessing (names of those for whom I pray).

Thank you for laughter, support, friendship and joy.

Thank you for peace, protection and freedom.

Thank you for good health of body, mind and spirit.

Thank you for opportunities to serve God to the best of my abilities.

Thank you for beauty and inspiration.

Thank you for the many sources of your spiritual guidance.

Thank you for your life, death, resurrection and ongoing presence in this world.

Thank you for these and for all of the many, abundant blessings of this life.

The list of blessings continues until the possibilities have been exhausted, as this stretches the mind beyond the finite borders of the problems at hand and generates a renewed sense of perspective about one's place in the larger scheme of things.

Praising leads to conscious gratitude, which sharpens awareness of the tiniest miracles so often taken for granted in everyday living –

a glorious flower emerging impossibly from a crack in a wall;

the meticulous handiwork of a bird's nest;

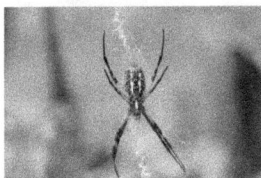

the splendor of a spider's web, glistening with dew at daybreak;

a turtle maneuvering safely across a busy road.

When daily praise becomes a habit, one begins to feel like part of a divine conspiracy for good; like a member of the "Heavenly Host" who exist to praise God and assist in the manifesting of that perfect love here on Earth. As the small miracles become more and more evident, so much more powerful and humbling is the grandeur of the galaxies' inexplicable beauty, balance and order.

We humans have been freely given everything we need to live here in total peace and harmony. Our planet is essentially the Garden of Eden, complete with more than enough resources to feed, clothe, shelter, nurture and respect one another as worthy benefactors of God's love. But every day we seem to "choose the apple" and demand self-gratification rather than that which would serve the greater good.

Every day we choose our will over the will of God, as though this magnificent Creator of the Universe could not possibly know what we need for happiness, growth and sustenance.

Daily, active praise and gratitude will reel the consciousness up out of the abyss of ego and place it on higher ground, in richer soil, in preparation for addressing God with our petitions.

CHAPTER TWO
PETITION

So I say to you, "Ask and you shall receive; seek and you shall find; knock and it shall be opened to you. For whoever asks, receives; whoever seeks, finds; whoever knocks, is admitted."
(Luke 11:9-10)

With our newfound appreciation for the immensity and glory of all creation, how can we possibly approach the Almighty Craftsman with our petty trials and tribulations? One of the pitfalls of giving praise and gratitude the "first place" position in the Active Meditation process is that we may feel guilty about asking for anything or even allowing our thoughts to drift into the needy or negative corridors of our minds. But trivializing the issues that cause us pain and inner conflict will ultimately create imbalance in our lives and make us less receptive to the blessings that are rightfully ours.

For me, the petitioning part of the process includes a broad range of requests, both global and personal. My petitions generally include some of the following:

Lord,
Please bless all who are suffering in any way – in body, mind or spirit, especially the children and vulnerable of this world.

Please bless all who are struggling with separation from your loving, healing presence for any reason; especially fear, loneliness, anxiety, violence or injustice.

Please bless the leaders of this world and help them to seek your guidance in all matters.

Please bless all whose needs are unmet and all who are in a position to meet them.

Please bless all who are trying to do God's will; grant them faith, hope, love and perseverance.

Please bless all who are not trying to do God's will; whose lives are ego-driven and hearts are filled with hatred. Help them to recognize your healing, guiding presence.

Please bless (names of loved ones and those for whom I've offered to pray).

Please help me to understand (current issues and concerns).

Please put me where you want me, Lord. Make my will one with yours. Help me to seek, clearly recognize, follow and trust your guidance in all things; and grant me the privilege of being an open and willing channel of your light and love, for your glory and the highest good.

I absolutely believe that all prayers are not only heard but answered, and no prayer is wasted. Sometimes the answer is not what we hoped for, and sometimes it feels as though we're praying into a huge vacuum. If true faith is believing without seeing, then prayer must be faith-based rather than outcome-based.

When we pray for the healing of a person, for example, we must assume that the healing power we invoke actually does go where it is most needed, whether we recognize it or not.

In our goal-oriented society we have come to define "healing" as "curing" – but they are not synonymous; we will all eventually shed these physical bodies. Perhaps our prayers for healing of the sick actually go to their spirits to help them prepare for death. Perhaps they go to the loved ones of the dying. But they do not go to waste and should, in fact, be expanded to include healing for families, communities, nations and the world.

Outcome-based prayer is another way of "choosing the apple" – of telling God that we know best about what we need. It sets us up for cynicism and disappointment. When I pray, "Put me where you want me, Lord; make my will one with yours" I am reminding myself that wherever I am at any given moment is neither an accident nor a detour. And then I head out into the world each day in a state of exhilaration – and a little trepidation – about the joys and challenges ahead.

Faith-based prayer, though not an invitation to live recklessly, does empower us to live fearlessly. While prayer is always clearly heard, the answers are not always clearly received by us; at least, not the ones we do not wish to hear. In these instances, the answer may be one of the following:

No.

Not at this time.

Not in this way.

Your spirit has asked for this challenge in order to learn and grow in some way.

This experience will eventually make perfect sense.

Be patient and trust in the plan.

You will understand my love for you when this is all over.

I believe that all of us, having been made "…in the image and likeness of God" (*"God created man in his image; in the divine image he created him: male and female he created them"* Genesis 1:27) are wired to be channels of the same pure, powerful love that flowed through Jesus Christ. Tales of the historical Jesus, and even the accumulated mythology surrounding his life story, point to a being who existed not to somehow flaunt his divinity and ability to perform miracles; but to model who we are. It was never about him; he never asked to be placed above his fellow travelers. His words were, *"Follow me,"* not *"Worship me."*

He prayed and meditated, relinquished his will to the will of the Father, and headed out into the world each day armed with the swords of faith, hope and love. Thousands of people followed, probably for thousands of reasons. And if we accept the traditional ending of this story, we believe that those whose prayers had been outcome-based cheered at the crucifixion of this man who did not fit their image of a messiah; while the people of faith wept, and waited for God's greater plan to be revealed.

This man, Jesus, must have possessed an amazing blend of charisma, intensity, good humor, wisdom, humility and strength to command such a diverse, enormous and enduring following. When he spoke, people from all walks of life listened and considered his words. Those who could not transcend the ball and chain of the human ego could neither believe nor follow. To love God and love our neighbor is a far more difficult calling than all of the other words in the Scriptures put together; and all of the transcribing, memorizing, quoting and righteous preaching that has ensued cannot change this most basic command.

The words to remember when the faith tank is running on empty are, *"And know that I am with you always, until the end of the world"* (Matthew 28:20). These are the words that lead me to invoke Christ in prayer and to believe that all prayer, great and small, is heard and answered.

Jesus' style of teaching is quite thought provoking, and actually led to the third part of the Active Meditation process. He did not simply lecture; he rarely criticized, and although all indications point to his being extremely articulate he never spoke condescendingly or used language that was beyond the comprehension of the common people. He called upon familiar images, delicately and skillfully weaving them into verbal tapestries that we refer to as "parables" so the people could visualize what he was saying and apply the images to their own lives in a practical way. Today we might say that his teachings were very "user friendly" – whether he was speaking to one person or thousands of people.

While the Pharisees and Sadducees dwelt primarily in the academic realm, referring to scholarly works and rules as a guide for living, Jesus brought the message down to the heart level. People could picture what he was saying as he spoke and conjure up those pictures later, in his absence, when they needed reminders of his teachings. He challenged them to see themselves as they could be, while loving them for who they were. He made them believe in their capacity to love, to do the right thing, to become something bigger than themselves – a community, a world connected in spirit and vision.

And so the third part of the Active Meditation process – after tilling and fertilizing the spiritual soil through praise and petition – is about mentally forming and "affirming" images of the resources and metaphors that will help us meet the challenges of *our* lives like our ancestors in faith. Affirmation and visualization helps us to believe, as Jesus does, that we can fully become that which we intuitively know ourselves to be.

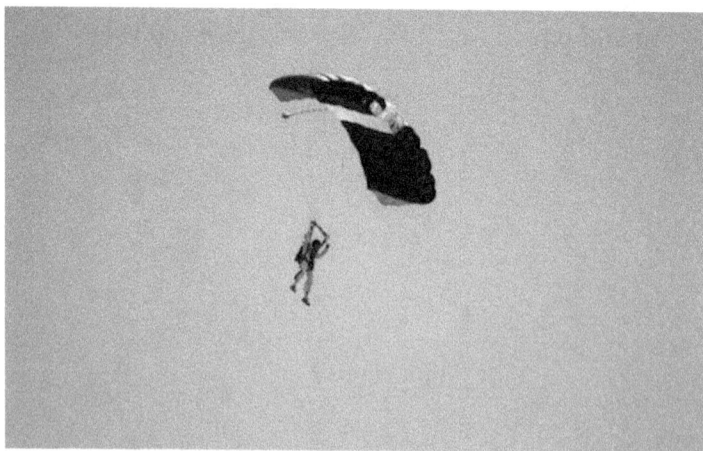

CHAPTER THREE
AFFIRMATION AND VISUALIZATION

In reply Jesus told them: "Put your trust in God. I solemnly assure you, whoever says to this mountain, 'Be lifted up and thrown into the sea,' and has no inner doubts but believes that what he says will happen shall have it done for him. I give you my word, if you are ready to believe that you will receive whatever you ask for in prayer it shall be done for you."
(Mark 11:22-25)

Probably the most challenging phrase in this verse from Mark is *"...if you are ready to believe..."* How often do we sabotage our dreams, goals and aspirations by succumbing to the nagging voices of our own insecurities?

And how can we possibly conjure up a clear image of an all-powerful, all-loving God within the fragile, splintered frame of own limitations? Over and over again we are challenged to turn from outcome-based to faith-based prayer.

An "affirmation" is basically a sentence we declare to ourselves as factual. Our brain latches onto key words and the subconscious – the busy manifestor -- works to create the reality of the sentence. Every day we pummel our brains with affirmations, mostly negative, and paint an inner picture of ourselves that is beamed out the to world. "I will not eat junk food today" is translated, internally, to "…eat junk food…" A better way of aspiring to that desired body would be to say, "I am slender and healthy."

When a visualization, or picture, is attached to the affirmation it becomes a powerful tool for generating that reality, for better or for worse. The brilliant educators who pioneered "Sesame Street" figured this out many years ago and several generations of children have learned to read, write, count and even develop appropriate behaviors through the repetition and reinforcement of words, songs and images.

Olympic athletes will often confirm that, throughout the years of grueling practice that led them to the top, they routinely reassured themselves of their ability and envisioned themselves performing perfectly. Unfortunately, the negative underbelly of our media and entertainment industry also uses affirmation and visualization techniques that result in self-loathing and hateful behavior by force-feeding our minds with words and images of violence, despair and degradation. The subconscious mind, which neither condones nor condemns, takes it all in either way and holds onto the information like the hard drive in a computer. But that is another issue for another time and forum.

Within the context of the Active Meditation process, affirmation and visualization become a method of practicing focused prayer; of making us "ready to believe" that great things can truly happen when we remove our inner doubts and put our trust in God – the latter being the most important key to success. When we pray, "Make my will one with yours" w e are acknowledging that we are not The Source but, rather, channels of The Source. We are boldly presenting our illustrated wish list but ultimately saying, "Thy will be done" just as Jesus did in the Garden of Gethsemane.

He advanced a little and fell to the ground praying that if
it were possible this hour might pass him by. He kept saying,
"Abba (O Father), you have the power to do all things.
Take this cup away from me. But let it be as you would
have it, not as I."
(Mark 14:35-36)

When I transition from petitioning to the Affirmation/ Visualization part of the process, I begin at the end; that is, I restate at least the three concluding petitions because they are the most important, and then I work back from there.

The challenge is to ignore that ugly little inner voice that undermines confidence at every turn. Like a kitchen sponge, our psyche seems to soak up all of the little criticisms that have ever been tossed our way and allows them to grow and fester like bacteria. When we try to make a clean start, it swipes those toxic droplets across our consciousness and leaves us feeling worse than when we started. "I am slender and healthy" is met with, "No you're not! Your fat and out of shape!"

And thus it goes with each attempt to rewrite our mental script. Every individual must come up with a visualization that conquers this saboteur over and over. I picture a little bug-like character sitting on my shoulder. When my affirmations are met with a negative response, I always fling that creature through the air with a mental flick of my fingers – resulting in the simultaneous benefits of removing the problem and making me laugh, tapping yet another pool of healing energy! A sampling of affirmations follows:

I am a willing channel of the light of Christ in thought, word and deed, for the glory of God and the highest good.

I seek, recognize, follow and trust guidance from Father, Son and Holy Spirit.

My will is one with the will of God and I am exactly where God wants me to be.

I am at peace with everyone in my life.

I am in perfect health of body, mind and spirit.

I am the very best (...friend, wife, mother, teacher, etc.) I can be.

I live every moment of every day in conscious gratitude.

The affirmations continue, with variations and elaborations according to current issues, specific concerns, personal or professional goals and global intentions. With every affirmation I generate a detailed, ideal mental picture and then release it to the universe like a balloon with a special message attached.

"Let go and let God" is not a trifling old cliché but, rather, a vital step in opening our spirit to the daily miracles of God's intervention in our lives. Some may think, "But couldn't all of this work without involving God? Maybe I can manifest the realities I want without subordinating myself to some God who may or may not exist." The answer is yes, it would work. People are creating their own realities every day by focusing on the things they want and think they need. But ego-driven affirmation and visualization can be precarious and limited in scope, like riding in the passenger seat of a car driven by a child; or viewing a magnificent sunrise through a tiny window. The expression, "Be careful what you wish for – you may get it" is steeped in psychological and spiritual wisdom!

Up until this point in the process, there has been monologue but not dialogue. We have unloaded, exhausted, and totally wrung out our hearts to the Lord and his celestial committees until, at last, the screen is blank; the mind is open, we are ready to listen.

CHAPTER FOUR
LISTENING

My son, to my wisdom be attentive,
to my knowledge incline your ear,
that discretion may watch over you,
and understanding may guard you.
(Proverbs 5:1)

Why is it that so many people think God quit speaking to us two thousand years ago? Current stories of God's active, powerful presence in people's lives are often met with snickers and rolling eyes, as if it could not be possible that the Creator would waste time communicating with ordinary folks. And yet, a close look at the Old and New Testaments reveals that God specifically chose simple, imperfect people through whom to reveal his glory and infinite love time and time again. Stories of Jesus' ministry are filled with unlikely and unsavory characters whose hearts were opened and lives were transformed as the "important" people looked on in disgust and disbelief.

Whether we interpret the Bible literally or metaphorically, the message is the same: there is a God who has loved us since the beginning of time, and this God manifests here on earth every day in many ways to help us survive the turmoil we precipitate through our individual and collective free will. There is apparently no corporate ladder to Heaven;

no exclusive contract that says some are more deserving of salvation than others because of accomplishment, prestige or a particular religious affiliation. *If you, with all your sins, know how to give your children what is good, how much more will our heavenly Father give good things to anyone who asks him!* (Matt 7:11). Anyone.

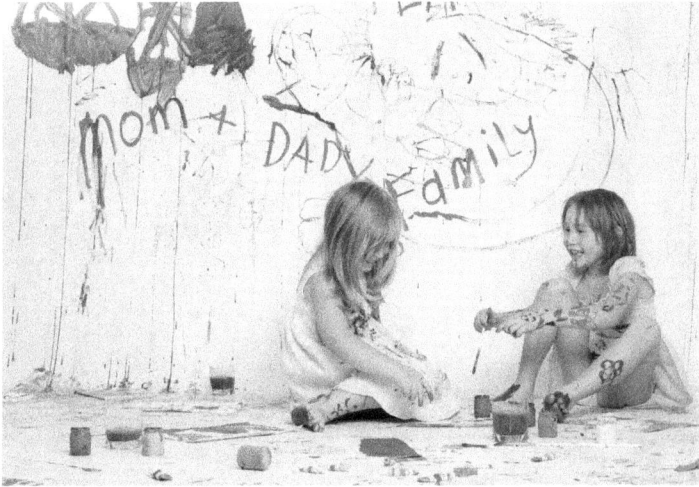

So often we ask the right questions, in the right spirit, for the right reasons; but then we do not trust the answers that come through our thoughts, dreams, intuitions and life experiences. Although there have been some documented cases of inexplicable, tangible responses from the great beyond, most of the time our communication with the Lord is subtle and only conscious faith can bring it into focus. As a Christian, if I feel unsure of the authenticity of the message, I need only hold it up to the integrity of Scripture to determine congruency or a lack of it. For example, if I were to pray for guidance regarding a stressful situation with a co-worker and my "intuition" told me to harm or humiliate that person in some way I would know this did not come from the Christ spirit but from my own wounded ego. The ability to listen with spiritual focus happens only when the inner chatter has been cleared away and we are, again, *"...ready to believe that (we) will receive whatever (we) ask for in prayer."*

Once we achieve this state of readiness, the messages begin to flow in amazing and often humorous ways. Sometimes it's a phrase from a song, running over and over through the mind; sometimes it's the exact words we needed to hear from another human being; sometimes it's a dream, a feeling, or even a personalized license plate on the car in front of us! And sometimes the answers appear as words within the frame around that internal screen where our visualizations appeared earlier in the process.

The challenge is to stay alert once a prayer request has been formulated and issued and to then move forward in faith when the response feels authentic. Ideally, the insights that occur during this time should be written down for later reflection. If time and circumstance do not allow – as when a revelatory moment occurs while driving – then we should at least make a very conscious mental note and integrate it into our larger body of spiritual guidance.

In the darkest times of the soul, when structured prayer seems impossible, we need only remember the words, again, *"...I am with you always, until the end of the world"* (Matt 28:20) and picture Christ enveloping the world in loving arms of light. In any case, the listening phase is absolutely essential for effective conclusion to the Active Meditation process. This is the time when the flowers emerge from the weeds; the simple melody is heard within the grand orchestration of the symphony; the scattered pieces of the puzzle come together to form a coherent picture.

CHAPTER FIVE
HOW SHALL WE PRAY?

One day he was praying in a certain place. When he had finished, one of his disciples asked him, "Lord, teach us to pray, as John taught his disciples."
(Luke 11:1)

The Lord's Prayer has been translated many ways, in many languages, including and deleting certain words and phrases from one version of the Bible to another. In most Christian gatherings, however, there seems to be an almost universal way of reciting it together, often while holding hands. We almost chant the familiar words, lulled into a comforting rhythm that can inadvertently prevent us from actually hearing what we are saying. I recently found myself in this state when, suddenly and with conscious clarity, I realized that this simple prayer totally encompasses all four parts of the Active Meditation process – although not necessarily in the order previously described.

Our Father who art in heaven, hallowed be thy name.

We offer **praise**, acknowledging the existence of God in heaven and the holiness of God's very name.

Thy kingdom come, thy will be done on earth as it is in heaven.

We **affirm** our belief that the Kingdom of God is at hand on earth – just as in heaven – when God's will has priority over our own. Whenever we say this part of the Lord's Prayer we automatically **visualize** God's perfect kingdom in our mind's eye.

Give us this day our daily bread,

We **petition** God to provide for our most basic needs – our "daily bread."

and forgive us our trespasses as we forgive those who trespass against us.

This **petition** should probably be uttered in a humble whisper, with the hope that God will not actually dole out forgiveness as shabbily as we do! We should sort of pray between the lines here, that God will forgive us far more generously than we forgive those who trespass against us. Forgiveness is an ongoing challenge that Jesus seems to have placed in the heart of this prayer to gently remind us that we are called to love and forgive over and over, *"...seventy times seven..."* (Matt 18:22).

And lead us not into temptation, but deliver us from evil;

This is both a **petition** and an **affirmation.** We ask God to provide strength and guidance as we face the temptations of the Garden of Eden in which we live. And we firmly believe that when we do succumb to these temptations God will deliver us safely from our messes and help us find ways to begin again.

For thine is the kingdom and the power and the glory forever, amen.

Although not part of the original Scripture, this standard conclusion beautifully returns to the opening words of **praise** and immediately places all of our hearts' desires into perspective.

According to Gospel writer Luke, when the disciples asked Jesus how to pray his typically wise and loving response was to provide a brief, functional prayer that could be applied anytime, anyplace, in any circumstances. How well he understood human nature! With our innate distractibility we want simple tools and instructions; like the disciples, we long for a quick and direct way to dialogue with the Creator about our life situations at any given moment.

When I had that lucid moment about the correlation of the Lord's Prayer to Active Meditation I experienced an almost urgent need to share this process with anyone and everyone who has searched for a means to improve spiritual communication. With the Lord's Prayer as the tool, these "instructions" truly can be applied anytime, anyplace, in any circumstances.

CHAPTER SIX
APPLICATION

When you are praying, do not behave like hypocrites who love to stand and pray in synagogues or on street corners in order to be noticed. I give you my word, they are already repaid.
(Matthew 6:5)

"I don't know how to pray."

"Prayer is not allowed where I work."

"I'm too busy to meditate."

"I don't even know if I believe in God – how can I pray?"

"I don't have time to pray."

The excuses for keeping God at a distance are endless. And yet, regardless of our religious or non-religious orientation there exists a deep and natural yearning within the human spirit for connection to something greater than ourselves. We long for a glimpse of the finished picture, to understand how the pieces fit together, to believe our lives have meaning. Why, then, do we constantly sabotage the quest for answers to the ancient questions embedded in our hearts?

The reason became clear to me while observing the behavior of a two-year-old child. As her parents offered assistance with some task that was clearly beyond her ability to perform alone, she folded her arms, planted her feet firmly in place and, with furrowed brow, declared, "I SELF!" The parents wisely allowed her to proceed, to a point, and then facilitated the next step in a way that would build resolve and muster trust. This team effort would morph into the building blocks of a sturdy foundation for self-confident, continued growth.

But only in a perfect world would children and parents communicate with such balance every time, and this world is far from perfect. Usually the child will say, "I SELF!" and then move forward with an ill-fated plan that ends in various degrees of disaster. The child does not have the ability to anticipate all of the potential outcomes; the cognitive understanding of "cause and effect" has not developed fully enough for the child to be able to predict what might happen as a result of a spontaneous action. But he or she knows absolutely for certain that outside help is not required.

As human beings in the grand scheme of God's universe, our level of evolution is probably equivalent to that of the two-year-old. Our limited spiritual cognition, combined with our human nature and God's gift of free will can be a deadly combination. Every time we stand firm and exclaim, "I SELF!" when opportunities for growth and discovery arise, we plant virtual land mines all along the path, catapulting us backwards at times and totally destroying parts of us at other times.

Although the scriptural quotes used throughout this book are taken from the Judeo-Christian traditions, the values ring true for almost every major religion: love, forgiveness, respect, recognition of an omnipotent Being and a journey toward reunion with that Being whose name varies from one culture to another. Yes, the teachings have been twisted, misinterpreted, modified, taken out of context and wrongly applied throughout the centuries; but in their pure and intended form they are never about self-centeredness or disconnection from others.

Whether or not we understand God as the Father named in the Holy Trinity or simply recognize God's loving presence in a ...*gentle whisper*...*, we can send out a prayer and it will get wherever it needs to go. Prayer can be a simple, "Thank you" when we barely avoid a collision with another car on the highway; it can be the word, "Help!" when we are feeling helpless; it can be mindful appreciation for things of beauty and inspiration, or shared grief that creates a sense of union, or healing laughter with friends and family. Prayer is simply the ability to move from, "I SELF!" to, "Lord, I invite and invoke you to dwell at the center of my life."

> *The LORD said, "Go out and stand on the mountain in the presence of the LORD, for the LORD is about to pass by." Then a great and powerful wind tore the mountains apart and shattered the rocks before the LORD, but the LORD was not in the wind. After the wind there was an earthquake, but the LORD was not in the earthquake. After the earthquake came a fire, but the LORD was not in the fire. And after the fire came a gentle whisper. When Elijah heard it, he pulled his cloak over his face and went out and stood at the mouth of the cave. (1 Kings 19:11-13)*

The Active Meditation process does not always need to be followed in its entirety; each part can help us in different situations. For example, praise and gratitude balance perspective when we find ourselves wallowing in anger, resentment or frustration. A simple, "Thank you, Lord, for this home" when we feel overwhelmed with endless chores; or "Thank you for family" when our energy is being stretched with family responsibilities; or "Thank you for the ability and opportunity to work" when exhausted by our jobs, generates a sort of spiritual chiropractic adjustment to our overall system in a matter of seconds.

CHAPTER SEVEN
CONCLUSION

Peter proceeded to address them in these words: "I begin to see how true it is that God shows no partiality. Rather, the man of any nation who fears God and acts uprightly is acceptable to him. This is the message he has sent to the sons of Israel, the good news of peace proclaimed through Jesus Christ who is Lord of all." (Acts 10:34-36)

I did go to graduate school and earn the M.Ed in Counseling that allowed me to enjoy fifteen wonderful years as an Elementary School Counselor. Active meditation helped me to revel in the blessings and weather the storms of that journey along with many other trials and tribulations along the way. As a self-appointed warrior for children, particularly the disadvantaged, I found solace and balance through these daily reminders of the Greater Plan. Consistent active meditation helped me to choose my battles carefully; to focus energy toward those that were "shown" to be priority issues.

Ironic as it may seem, during my time as a counselor in the public-school system I never could jump on the prayer-in-schools bandwagon because I believe we can already pray wherever we are, whenever we want. Prayer naturally blossoms from the heart when the seeds of faith have been planted and nurtured. When children are taught from Day One to integrate conversations with God into their daily routine, faith becomes a guiding force behind perspectives and choices, and the resulting positive behaviors inspire and pique the curiosity of peers. In my experience, alienating those who disagree with us or verbally thrashing others with out-of-context scriptural verses has a counterproductive effect on building the Kingdom of God. If public school prayer were enforced, whose prayers would they be? And who, in this country that prides itself on liberty and justice for all, would feel disenfranchised? To quote Peter again, *"I begin to see how true it is that God shows no partiality."*

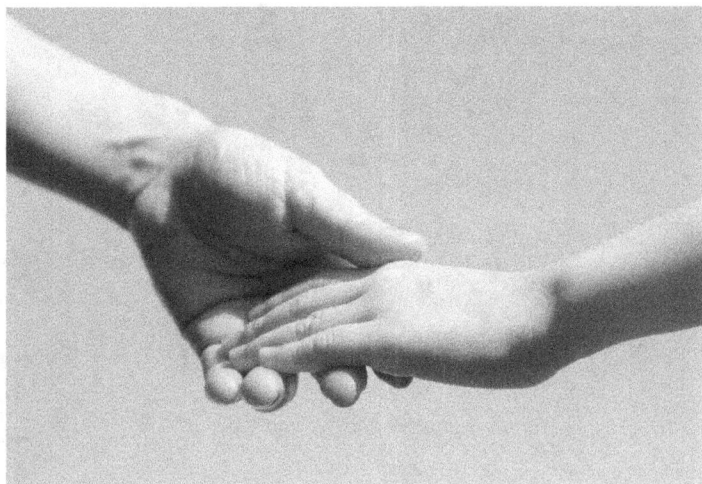

While books may have conclusions, physical life does not conclude until the final exhalation. Having been raised by parents who fully embraced life to the very end, I was never inclined to resign myself to the stereotyped image of "slowing down" with age. In my fourteenth year as a school counselor I felt the winds of change rustling in my soul and, although I had been doing abbreviated forms of the Active Meditation process regularly, I began the daily walks once again to gather strength of focus and clarity of vision. I had been fussing for years about the lack of a local place where people could grab a quick, healthy meal without having to deal with tobacco smoke, alcohol or the wasted time and money of a full-service restaurant. An opportunity arose to open such a place myself. With no restaurant experience, limited financial resources, the blessing of my husband and a load of faith I embarked upon a new career as many of my friends were preparing for retirement.

Once again I found assurance that when we listen with faith and focus we discover that God is constantly speaking to us just as surely as television, radio and WiFi signals continue to broadcast whether our equipment is on or off. I followed the guidance with the aforementioned exhilaration/trepidation and found myself, against all odds, owning and operating a healthy café in partnership with my very gifted, business-oriented daughter and a fabulous staff of teens and young adults. The years of school counseling experience kicked into overdrive as I collaborated with local high school teachers in workforce development efforts and helped students juggle the options awaiting them after graduation; and I will always cherish the humbling privilege of accompanying those kids through the thorny, rocky trails of adolescence. I knew I had made the right decision in opening the café when an elderly female customer called me aside one day, chatted for a few moments with twinkling eyes that deeply searched my own, and finally informed me, "I knew this was a blessed business as soon as I walked in."

Thanks to that outstanding, enthusiastic group of young employees, the café established itself as a fun and friendly community destination and the Holy Spirit found a way to ease me out of there and turn it over to new owners – another "quantum leap" – for the next adventure. I reconnected with a former school counseling friend and we opened a little practice offering life-coaching skills to people of all ages. The unique image on that big jigsaw puzzle of our lives seems to emerge over time as seemingly random life experiences fall into place, one after another, like puzzle pieces exactly where they are meant to be.

What will be next? I cannot say I know, but I can say with confidence that I will be wherever I am supposed to be. There is always a clear and purposeful path when we ask the Lord to hold the lantern before us. The view of our little world and all its triumphs and troubles has often been compared to a tapestry, with God's view on the side of the finished picture and humanity able to see only the massive, tangled underside of crisscrossing threads and confusing patterns. Faith is the intuitive and unconditional belief in the Designer of this grand masterpiece; and knowing without a doubt that every, single thread contributes a vital component to the magnificent panorama. Every life, every experience, every choice we make impacts and is connected to every other in some way that will all fit together and make perfect sense when we see it from the other side.

Beginning each day with an invocation of Christ in *Praise*, *Petition*, *Affirmation/Visualization* and *Listening* empowers us to move forward fearlessly; to find him in all people and recognize when his guiding presence is embracing us. We are spiritually buckling up, fully prepared and looking forward to whatever lies ahead. And, in this state of readiness, every moment of every day the Kingdom of God is emerging within and around us, little by little, on earth as it is in heaven.

NOTES

Notes

Notes

Notes

Active Meditation for Manifesting the Kingdom

Notes

_____

_____

_____

_____

_____

_____

_____

_____

_____

_____

_____

_____

_____

To contact the author about ordering multiple copies of
this book for your church or book club, or scheduling
Celie for speaking engagements, please visit her website:
www.themainchannel.net

www.ingramcontent.com/pod-product-compliance
Lightning Source LLC
LaVergne TN
LVHW021543080426
835509LV00019B/2812